Laurence Bowen

See our other products!

THIS BOOK BELONGS TO

blank pages between
illustrations prevent colors
from showing through to
the next picture

blank pages between
illustrations prevent colors
from showing through to
the next picture

blank pages between
illustrations prevent colors
from showing through to
the next picture

blank pages between
illustrations prevent colors
from showing through to
the next picture

blank pages between
illustrations prevent colors
from showing through to
the next picture

blank pages between
illustrations prevent colors
from showing through to
the next picture

blank pages between
illustrations prevent colors
from showing through to
the next picture

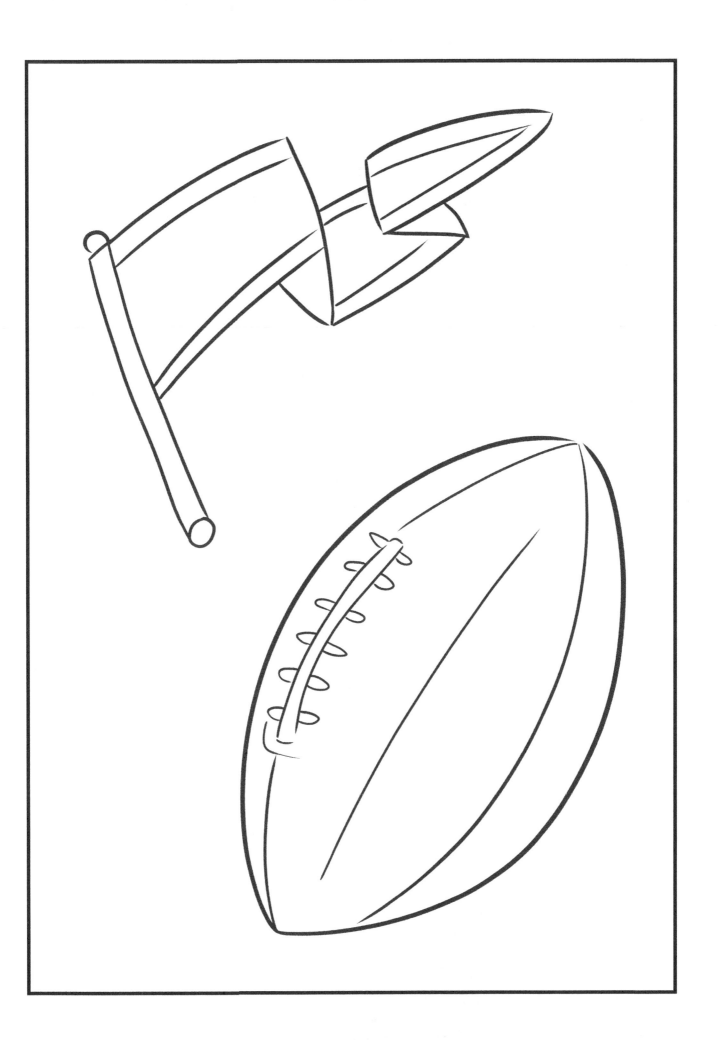

blank pages between
illustrations prevent colors
from showing through to
the next picture

blank pages between
illustrations prevent colors
from showing through to
the next picture

blank pages between
illustrations prevent colors
from showing through to
the next picture

blank pages between
illustrations prevent colors
from showing through to
the next picture

blank pages between
illustrations prevent colors
from showing through to
the next picture

blank pages between
illustrations prevent colors
from showing through to
the next picture

blank pages between illustrations prevent colors from showing through to the next picture

blank pages between
illustrations prevent colors
from showing through to
the next picture

blank pages between
illustrations prevent colors
from showing through to
the next picture

blank pages between
illustrations prevent colors
from showing through to
the next picture

blank pages between
illustrations prevent colors
from showing through to
the next picture

blank pages between
illustrations prevent colors
from showing through to
the next picture

blank pages between
illustrations prevent colors
from showing through to
the next picture

blank pages between
illustrations prevent colors
from showing through to
the next picture

blank pages between
illustrations prevent colors
from showing through to
the next picture

blank pages between
illustrations prevent colors
from showing through to
the next picture

blank pages between illustrations prevent colors from showing through to the next picture

blank pages between
illustrations prevent colors
from showing through to
the next picture

blank pages between
illustrations prevent colors
from showing through to
the next picture

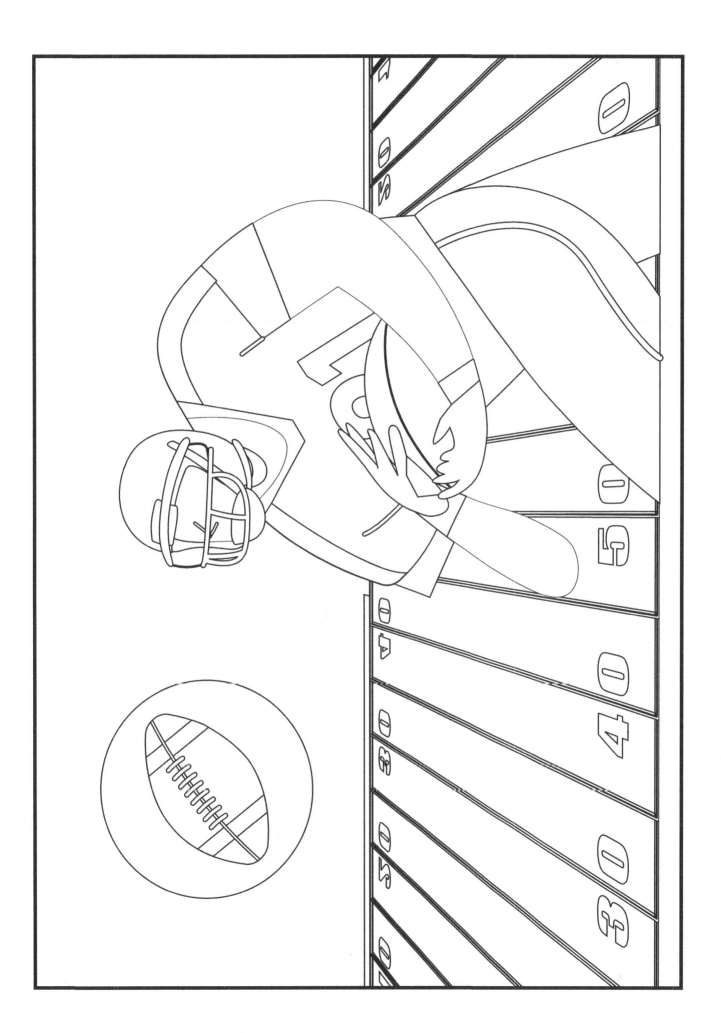

blank pages between
illustrations prevent colors
from showing through to
the next picture

blank pages between
illustrations prevent colors
from showing through to
the next picture

blank pages between
illustrations prevent colors
from showing through to
the next picture

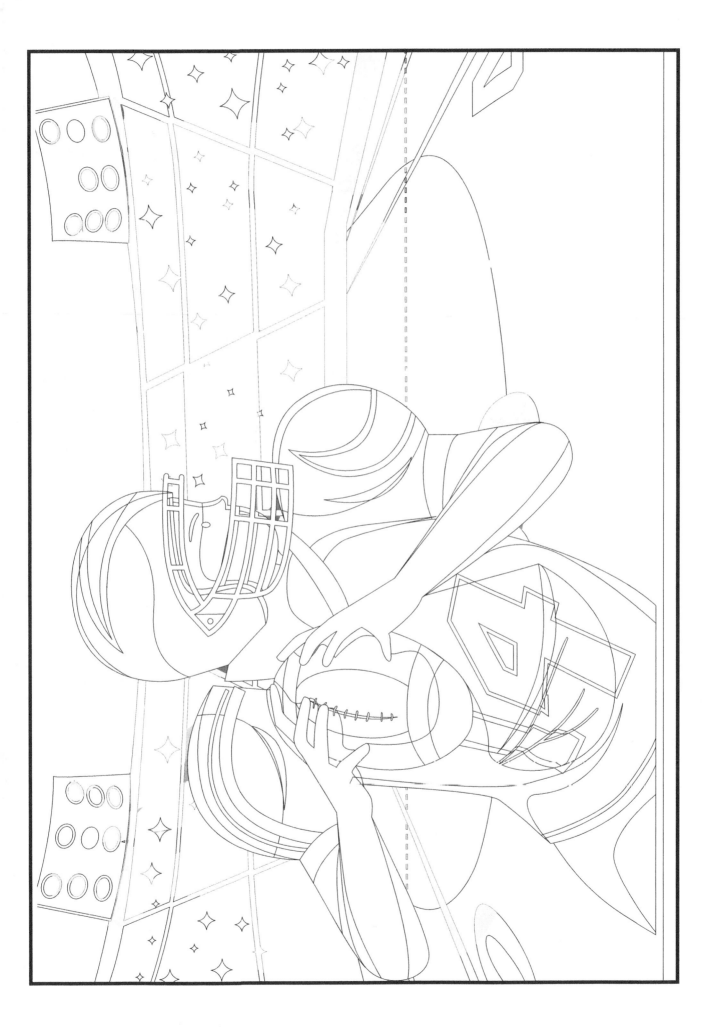

blank pages between
illustrations prevent colors
from showing through to
the next picture

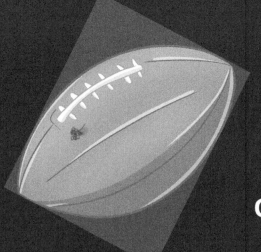

One last thing...

We would love to hear your comments about this book.

If you liked this book or found it helpful, we would appreciate it if you would post a short review on Amazon. Your support makes all the difference and we personally read all reviews.

If you would like to leave a review, just click on the review link on the Amazon page for this book.

We thank you for your support.

Made in the USA
Las Vegas, NV
08 December 2023

82306638R00037